LETTERS OF A

CRIMINAL

POETRY BY

ROBERT G. ANSTEY

For Yvonne without who's encouragement
& constant prodding this project would
never have gotten off the ground & who's
affection has been the major inspiration
& made being a "criminal" more acceptable.

LETTERS OF A

CRIMINAL

POETRY BY

ROBERT G. ANSTEY

ISBN 0-9697494-0-6

First printing August 1993

Published by:
West Coast Paradise Publishing
P.O. 43147
Richmond Centre P.O.
Richmond B.C.
V6Y 3Y3

Front cover photo by the author.
Back cover photo by Yvonne Lee.

Canadian Cataloguing in Publication Data

Anstey, Robert G. (Robert Graham), 1949-
 Letters of a Criminal : poetry

 I.Title
PS8551.N884L4 1993 C811'.54   C93-091741-3
PR9199.3.A588L4 1993

INDEX

INDEX CON'T

Other Forthcoming Titles By
Robert G. Anstey

- Everything Was Fine Til The Puppy Died
- Canadian Dreamland Vol. 1
- Canadian Dreamland Vol. 2
- Black Sheep

SHE'S IN PAIN

She's in pain
at the sound of a name
from my distant past,
the thought of a dream
that didn't last,
somewhere back
long years ago,
every move where she
was not included,
every day when
she was not there,
she's in pain
when I'm not there
and cannot be
because of some
previous commitment,
maybe I am looking
somewhere else
& not at her,
she's in pain
when dreaming
of some other situation
when we're apart
& she is left to wait
those long moments
when we're together again,
she's in pain
when days are long
& someone else has taken
my time & attention,
she remembers what its like
for us to be
just two - under covers
warm & tight,
snuggled in the night
far away from everyone
& everything that
would remind her
of those days
when she's in pain.

1

QUALITY PEOPLE

You surround yourself
with people who
have feelings deep
& hearts true
sentimental, yes
emotional too,
people who have lived
& felt the pain of life,
felt it's sting,
they have touched
a measure of sorrow
in their lives
& today people talk to you,
not empty words
or joking banter
but words that touch
down in your heart
where you know they've been,
some have lived
long years,
carried a weight
of pain behind
& yet they lift their face
& smile at you
& feel your pain
& understand that
what you feel
is hard for you.
You love to speak
a word or two
to people who,
like you,
know that life is not
just fun & games
but hard times too,
they lift you up
when you are down,

quiet nerves,
reassure your mind
& let you know
that they are there
when you fall & need
a friend.

BENEATH THE RUBBLE

Beneath the rubble in a life left behind,
fragments & bits of broken dreams
& things that could have been
lay moldering in piles long forgotten,
a memory here encapsulated in time
when all around has changed & gone,
a missed chance there that could
have changed the course of history,
buried long ago in the rush & scurry
of an everyday life.

Beneath the rubble in a life left behind,
fond times lay scattered here & there,
littered randomly at inadvertent moments,
never planned, sometimes surprises,
but all too short because there were
always black times that overshadowed them,
digging down into the rubble is
sometimes a messy business,
you never know what your hand
will bring up.

Beneath the rubble in a life left behind
there stands a structure still today
whose attic trunks are full of yesterday's
things, things that made life go back then,
cobwebs dangle & wiggle when the lid is raised
& deep inside regrets pile high
& all the sorrows that come from them
leave creases in faces of those
who hold them dear.

SOMETHING ABOUT LIBRARIES

There's something about libraries
that makes you want
to go to the bathroom,
the heat perhaps
or the closeness,
all those books,
the people - arms laden
with weighty manuals
of knowledge,
silent whispers - secrets,
or a long lost book
now found,
excitement at the prospect
of reading the unopened pages,
anticipation of the
truth uncovered.
There's something about libraries
makes you want to
plunk down in a corner
with a good book
& spend the day,
trouble is - when you find
the number of the book you want
& then you find the location
of the book you want
& then you find that someone
else has already
taken it out.

KON-TIKI

A new day crawls slowly
up the eastern sky,
on a balsa raft
far out to sea
six men alone with the world
padding softly from log to log,
gazing westward
in the path of the sun-god,
blue-green waves like buildings
in endless swells
rock them, shake them,
push them on their journey,
out of touch with the bustling
world of cars & people
but right in touch with
the harmony of nature,
endless blue horizon
all around & all above
& bottomless fathoms
down below,
sea life in all their shapes
& colours & each with his own
way of life,
one eats another & another
his brother
& life goes on,
the six guests peer cautiously
into this world
with half fear & half awe
at the vastness of it all
& delight in the serenity
& peace (because, after all,
this is how it's supposed to be),
man in God's creation,
harmonizing with it
(not killing it),
the drift & pull
& current & wind
carry this little speck

of insignificance
far beyond time & reality
& thoughts of home are far away,
one day the strange
& foreign sound
of a pounding surf
touches ears & beats hearts
& the welcome sight
of sea birds feasts eyes
& soon the tropics
in all their splendor
are upon them,
palm trees wave them all ashore,
the sun-god beckons
them onto hot, white sand
& stars-a-million
bid them sleep
with nostrils full
of green sea air
tinged with foliage, earth
& bone dry wood
& natives brown with
ivory teeth
laugh & dance & toss
them all a welcome mat
& sadly wave them all good-bye
as the journey ends
& they lose their new-found friends,
the sun-god crawls back down
the western sky
to wave his own good-bye,
balsa logs are hauled
back home
twisted & bent but with
wonderful thoughts & memories
of miles of ocean,
gallons of sea
& long days basking
in Neptune's garden.

NO ONE KNOWS THE PAIN SHE'S SEEN

No one knows the pain she's seen
or looks inside to see the sorrow,
no one knows the irony
or sees the empty reason
for why she walks the streets today
when yesterday she held
in hands well accustomed to
looking after things
a position which would last
for years
& keep her satisfied.
No one knows the pain she's seen
when worlds went spinning,
turning round
& left her wondering
why this friend evaporated
& that one disappeared
& all the handles that she held
gave way & left her dangling,
pockets dry & stomach growling
when before it was no problem
buying this & that & paying
the piper when he called.
No one knows the pain she's seen
when endless doorways need unlocking
& knuckles cold from constant knocking
leave a distant island sort of feeling
like no one else will ever know
& lonely creeping starts from
feet & works to bone & marrow
& soon the motive for this life is gone,
passers-by & nothing-faces never
see the soul inside.
No one knows the pain she's seen
when rainbows sprang out ahead
in all their splendor

& then all-in-a-flash they went,
the well-laid plans went along too
for the ride,
friends/aquaintances & long-time
work-mates all a memory
& people think she's A-OK,
not a problem in the world.
But no one knows the pain she's seen
when light does not appear at the end
of the long, long tunnel
the way its supposed to,
when promises fail & enthusiasm wanes,
(people say they will when they won't
& that they do when they don't)
& she covers it so well to some
(but others know)
that this pain she's seen is deep & real
& won't go away til
it's had it's fill.
No one knows the pain she's seen,
she can't go here & can't go there,
what would they think?
& how would she feel?
this takes money & that takes cash
& he wants his & she wants hers
& what's left for all those
things she's got to have?
it's a pain that few can know
because few are sitting there today,
the rainbow's gone & this
searching heart goes on
& no one knows the pain.

BEWARE THE FIREY WARRIOR

Beware the firey warrior
wielding a sword & threatening me,
righteous to the end,
I've fallen short again,
stumbled & fallen again,
failed & gone off-track again
& so the firey warrior
is on my back again.
Beware the firey warrior
who appears when you are down
at your lowest,
sitting lonely on your island,
the righteous sword is swinging
& you'd better keep away
lest you get caught
& stung once again.
Beware the firey warrior
who sits & waits for you to fall
& when you do
he'll be right there sword in hand,
wagging finger - shaking head,
keep him far away from me
this firey warrior
with his righteous sword.

NEVER HAD THE CHANCE

Never had the chance to
simply sit & ponder
by myself alone
without worrying about others
& what they're doing now,
maybe some problem has arisen
& I must jump up & go,
never had the chance to be
myself & think alone
without some voice
appearing saying why
or what is that you're doing?
shouldn't you be doing
something else for me?
Never had the chance
to just be me,
others had to come first,
they needed something done,
but now the chance to sit
alone has come,
to scan the mirror warily
& find out what
that object is
staring back at me,
never had the chance
to see that thing before,
it's new & different & it wants
to understand some more.

FOREST NIGHT

Evening set it's latest sun
on down among the trees,
no one sees the darkness settle
somewhere off in yonder woods,
blanket covers heads & hearts
& silence peers into the cold,
fear creeps boldly now that
all his friends are here,
lonely hidden halfway between
rocks & brush & dirt & staring
up into a stone black night,
not another living creature
shows his face at me tonight,
toes wiggle desperate for warmth,
heart beats out the rythym
of it's own symphony
while waiting impatiently for
the thought that maybe soon
dawn is coming to release
& set me free,
But now the running moment
seems to cling on me like mud
& time jumps slo-mo like
that dream I had
& I ask no one who is always here
where is dawn & why is she so long?
I will never be the same
if she doesn't soon come reaching
to me like my lover in the night,
I will shiver & become no more
than leaves from last autumn,
I will wait some short time soon
& close my ears to the crying
chorus invisible but all-too-near
& hope that maybe soon another
friend will overtake me,
he has come at times before
when pain & fear were all too near
& now I wait in silent haste

for me to fall into his waiting arms
where I will not see & hear & feel
til dawn comes filtering slowly
with those fingers through my eyelids
& brings her bright joy to me
once more.

HOW CAN EVERYTHING BE WRONG?

You taught me that
this was wrong & that was too,
& brought me from a world
of dreams and hopes,
taught me that those
dreams were wrong,
that they'd lead me astray,
away from all that's right,
taught me that my talents
were better supressed
because if they were not controlled
they would lead to shame,
you taught me that everything
I lived & hoped for was wrong,
but how can everything be wrong?
You taught me that
my self expression
was worldly & wrong,
that it would make me worldly too
& that things that were normal
were really unnatural & wrong
though everybody did it
it was still wrong,
you taught me that
if I had this "thing" in my home
that I should hang my head in shame
because others would see it
& know that I was worldly,
you taught me that
if I didn't read the book
every day that I would starve,
all other books were wrong,
you taught me to sit
quietly in my chair
for hours at a time,
too much excitement was wrong,
but how can everything be wrong?
You taught me that to laugh
& think were wrong,

14

& some even suggested that
some foods were wrong
& in eating them I would get sick,
you taught me that
to sing those songs was wrong,
to wear that coat was wrong,
to have that friend was wrong,
to be a living, loving human
was wrong,
you taught me that
my neighbour was wrong,
I couldn't eat with him,
he would influence me
& make me more like him
but how can everything be wrong?
You taught me that
if my brother does not not
tow the line
then he is wrong
& I cannot speak to him
or I will be wrong too,
you taught me not to show
my children the world
or they would be warped
& end up wrong,
you taught me to take
my whole past life
& throw it all away
because it had only been
wrong & a waste of time,
that the locusts had eaten it,
but how can everything be wrong?
You taught me that
the man on the street
in all his ignorant ways
was wrong
& I was better than him,
you taught me to
look down on him,
feel sorry for him,
have pity on him,

because I was not wrong
like him,
you taught me to
tolerate him but
keep him at a distance,
you taught me that
my home was a place
where the dirt of the world
doesn't come
because I stop it at the door,
but how can everthing be wrong?
You taught me that
to fight is wrong,
to back down is better,
to be right is most important
whether I win or lose,
if I cause distractions
or raise problems
then I am wrong,
if I walk a fine line
& look good
then I am ok
but if I fail then I am wrong,
you taught me lots of things
& today I wonder as I look
back at all those years
how good my teacher was
& why is there all these tears
if I have walked so right
& worked so hard
at not being wrong?
why have so many
come & gone?
perhaps they asked like me today
how can everything be wrong?

MAN, THE MASTER

It used to be these rocks
& trees
had lives to live
& were left at peace,
but man has come with
motors, buildings & his great
dreams of progress,
tearing down & building up,
Man, the master of the universe
clearing land to
accomodate himself,
making room for himself
he fills the land
& fills the beaches,
fills all of earth's
outer reaches
till now no room remains
for fish & birds & animals,
trees become fallen relics,
mountainside dotted here & there
with houses,
Man, the master of it all
crashes through the wilderness
& leaves his trail of commotion
& distruction,
in his hand he holds the reins
to change things as he likes
but power makes him
stamp out life
& create huge garbage dumps
in every corner of the world.
Find a little spot away from him
this monster chewing up
the forests & the trees,
his progress & inventions
creating more problems
than he had before,
these rocks can tell the story,
their tears describe the days
when nature had its way

17

trees housed the birds,
the seas held the fish,
the land pushed the seedlings out,
today you stumble down
well-worn paths
strewn with candy wrappers,
signs of man's betrayal
of the land he takes
& uses for his pleasure,
the birds cannot decide
on the future of the earth,
neither can the animals,
they all await their master
to see what he will do,
is he a kind & gentle man
restoring all their beauty?
or is he the kind to rape & plunder
tearing up their only world?
they accept whatever happens,
whatever he will do,
not because it doesn't matter
but because they have no choice.

YOUR MUSIC

The beautiful sounds
of your flowing music
drift over me & sends
it's magic into my marrow,
like a drug it drifts me
softly into tomorrow,
goose-bumps & tingling
sensations run freely
& joyfully down my back,
the harmonies intermingle
& send me gently into
the atmosphere,
somewhere outside the universe
where I never see or feel
the bumps & jolts of life,
this is as close to heaven
that this earth can come,
your music leaves me
limp as laundry,
lying awake, but dreaming,
hoping no one will touch me
& end this feeling of being
brushed with the down
of a soft goose feather.

CHUNK OF LIFE

You have taken a
chunk of my life,
moulded it & changed it
like a chunk of marble
chiseled & polished
until it shines &
decorates some hallway,
like a chunk of cheese
sitting in the middle
of a cracker
adding colour & flavour
to a plate of horsd'oeuvres,
you have overwhelmed
this chunk of my life
with your love,
lifted it from rigid
formalities & routines,
mixed in your colours
& brightened it with your smile,
have patience with me because
I have been many years without you,
this chunk has rough edges
that need the smoothing
of your loving trowel
& the understanding
of your touch.

BALANCE

Sometimes the road between
ecstasy & suicide
is very slim,
like insanity & genius
the line is thin,
one moment contented
& smiling,
(for all the world
a happy man)
& the next moment
there is no bottom lower
& no emptiness deeper,
the space between the two
is life itself,
the real living, breathing
world of beating hearts
& swelling lungs,
the fire which keeps this
lamp alight & this
heart pulsing is
the love way beneath the skin,
unseen & unheard but
keeping the balance
between the two.

PROGRESS REPORT

Waiting out the time
while stress hangs wet-rag-like
over drooping shoulders
pulling down & weighing like
some ball & chain
& nagging headache burns
slowly back of head while
chest heaves seeking some
relief from tightness &
a cramping pain,
it is only three o'clock,
the day has worn away
some hours ago,
a whole week's work behind
me now,
the tension eases slowly
as nightfall creeps in
& this old day ebbs away,
night brings it's peace
& calm & quiet,
brain begins to function again,
relaxation from a grinding
world of decisions &
things-to-do,
time now to let that wet rag
dry out & flutter away
because tomorrow it returns again
to clamp down hard
it's grip of steel
holding in it's teeth
the time & movement of the day,
a tree is needed (or maybe two),
grass & leaves green & sweet
to spread their fragrance
into nostrils down inside,
fresh & free
they bring their peace where
stress before had torn apart.

EMILY

From off in a quiet neighbourhood
in a sleepy town in sleepy times
you walked alone & sought to
colour the shifting pictures
in your mind,
to depict the deepest spiritual
meaning caught away in a
dark & forboding forest,
the life that poured forth from
the giants of the woods
& what they said as they
towered over the sandy beaches
& the pounding sea
& what they thought from seeing
eyes that watched the world
from ages past.
It may have been easier
had someone taken an interest
& not laughed when they saw
the creations that you laboured over,
but they didn't understand,
maybe in a different day
or a different sleepy town...
your faced hard times
alone,
no one there to comfort except
the dogs & monk,
its easy today for us
to see your vision & talent
& to imaginarily prod you on,
("Go, Emily, go! Paint on!")
but we weren't there & even if
we were
we wouldn't have understood either,
you dreamed alone
& saw the totems, mountains against
the sky & heard them cry
& gave them life in colours
& strokes that wrenched their
true-life feelings up from the dead

23

you sat alone & dreamed
ran with dogs on Beacon Hill,
dug clay from Dallas cliffs
& formed from memory the images
brought from northern villages,
sisters turned cold shoulders
& high-taught tea-totallers
shrugged & turned to more
important things,
their paintings of bowls of roses
like photographs & postcards
void of any artistic quality
but satisfactory to thier own
untrained eyes.
Today Victoria still forgets you,
they still live as though you
never were,
cyclers ride past your house
in neon shorts & headbands
& most never heard your name,
it's all changed now, Emily,
you would not recognize the streets
& houses
& old Beacon Hill is all built up,
they try to cut down so many trees
& people are everywhere,
if you lived here now, you'd move,
the House is here but so much
has changed,
they have your gallery & they
use your name as if
you were their own,
but I wonder if its you they want
or the money they can make from you,
your books are here
full of the memories you carried
from years of wandering,
we read of all those familiar
places & feel the wind
of days gone by

it makes us sad that so much
has changed & gone,
swept away by time & the
ravages of progress,
indifferent people carelessly
throw the treasures of the past
behind them in their haste
to make another dollar
& in so doing they remove
their culture & become more hardened
& more calloused & less human
than people in your day,
sitting at your graveside
amoungst the whispering trees
it all comes back,
even though we were not there
you have brought it back,
you have given that time & feeling
back to us & taught us with your art
& your words & your inspiration,
we tread softly afraid to wake you,
afraid to let you see
what we've become,
if you were sad before at what your
eyes saw then
today the world would grieve you,
so sleep on, Emily & listen to
the sounds of totems preserved
by your hand,
gratefully acknowledgeing your
insight & imagination
that gave this world another
shot of inspiration
to see what isn't seen with
naked eye or education.

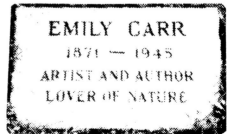

EMILY CARR
1871 — 1945
ARTIST AND AUTHOR
LOVER OF NATURE

WINDS OF LIFE

Whatever happens - let it be
under moon or stars
the world still turns,
at times it tumbles, shakes you,
takes you in it's arms & breaks you
but you stand again to fight again,
alone sometimes & prone sometimes
to pain & sorrow,
but never let it end the dream,
people come & people go,
they touch you once & sometimes twice,
they bump you here & nudge you there,
you get from them what good they have
whether youth or age,
deepest love or fits of rage,
you drink it all & take it in
& it all affects your deepest soul,
makes you man or mouse,
a begger or a king
& in the end
you'll thank them,
in the end,
because -
there always is one.

SOMEONE TO HANG OUT WITH

It wasn't lots of dollars
that I really had in mind,
a bank account that made me feel
that I was something special
or the power to yell & have
somebody jump for me,
it was not people bowing down to me
that would have made my day,
all I really wanted was
someone to hang out with.
It was not people looking up to me
regarding me with awe
or people seeking out a chance
to pry my wisdom loose
or shake my hand respectfully,
help me when I need someone
or share a meal with me,
give me all their old, used things
or tell me I'm a real good guy,
they always treated me with kindness
& smiled when I came around
but what I really would have liked
was somone to hang out with.

OLD LIFE/NEW LIFE

Engulfed in flames
escape is quick
but little remains
the public blames
insurance claims
& no one gains.

Return is short
forgot my hat
the walls are flat
everything is black
nothing but a smoky shack
get out quick & don't come back.

We move again
rebuild with wood & glue
a home, a house, some kind of view
in pink or red or green or blue
doesn't matter if it's new
long as there is me & you.

Voices in the dark
unseen bring fear
strange sounds are far too near
someone's had too much beer
it's just these new surroundings here
in time we hope the fog will clear.

IN THE GLINT OF A BRIGHT
SUMMERS DAY

In the glint of a bright summer's day
you sat, shoulders hunched clutching
a book in hands well-darkened
by the sun
squinting lightly, eyes fending off the power
of it's prodding spear.

In the glint of a bright summer's day
in lush green grass,
cool to the touch
tickling legs & other bare spots,
you munched ice cold ice cream,
looking off to traffic
flying past & listening
to voices shouting summer sounds.

In the glint of a bright summer's day
high on a rock basking like the seals
overlooking Howe Sound
in all it's beauty
breathing in the sea
& drinking deeply
the life-giving scent
of huge fir trees.

In the glint of a bright summer's day
you stood on deck
gripping the forestay
of a white sailboat, keeping balance,
keeping lookout,
loving every wispy breeze,
smiling quietly at your good fortune
that winter's cold is gone
leaving you surrounded by such beauty
to enjoy
in the glint of a bright summer's day.

29

THE HOUSE

It was an old house
(always had been old)
all wood & spiders
but it housed down below
in labyrith basement
a teeming business
full of hustling & bustling
where sons & parents
filled orders & in a quaint way
did all the things that
had to be done,
the house was the central point
to all of life then,
the umbilical cord that stretched
longer & longer as we
drifted away one by one
to new lives leaving
this centre that had
mothered us so long.
When it sold it was a fond farewell
we paid as we stripped it clean
of all it's dignity
leaving the shell for the new owner
to redress & outfit in new finery.

REMEMBERING THE PAST

I remember standing lonely
outside those double-doors
with suit & tie
greeting one & another
but feeling down inside
so lonely & all alone,
no one could share
the feelings of my heart
or touch the things I thought,
I felt it fruitless to explain
the changes down inside of me,
no one could really know it anyway,
each went to his own crowd
& talked their own language
& if you had someone to laugh
& talk with
you had a friend & were
far off better than I.
I remember pacing pavement
wasting time & yearning
for another moment spent with you,
glancing anticipatively
at streets & cars driving by
that maybe one of them were you
& wondering why it had to be
that I was here in agony
& you were there the same as me.
I remember feeling empty
& wondering what was happening,
the people all around
seemed to be still the same
as many years ago,
stuck in a moment of time,
& I sprung on ahead
& looking back & seeing
same old faces, same old smiles,
hearing same old phrases,
& glancing streets again
seeing you & I

alone in a world created
just for us.
I remember walking pensively
around parked cars,
searching out a friendly face
& a friendly ear,
but all I ever got it seemed
was idle chit-chat weather-talk,
these ones live their own life
& those live in their own world,
we had ours too, I suppose,
but broken fragments all around
each clinging to a common bit
of solid ground,
sometimes the lines so thin
& yet some cling for years on end,
& here I was seeing what had been
a solid ground for me
crumbling & tearing at the edges
& I was not clinging any longer.
I remember listening casually
to those so-familiar sounds,
mothers & babies,
fathers & young sons,
each smiling brightly & carefully,
well aware of others standing by
with approving nods & grins,
this listening seemed to jog my mind
& sadness seemed to enter in,
the will to fight was gone,
to try & be somebody else's
success story
wasn't worth it anymore,
I had those days & nights with you
that made me leap into another world
where none of those things
mattered anymore,
a new fresh breeze was wafting
past the window now,

32

the sounds were sweet & gentle,
compelling me in such a way I knew
there was no question
& there was no choice.

UNDERNEATH THE DOUBT

You never mean
a heartless cruelty,
to cause pain or
see an aching heart
but only move in
easy circles
doing what has to
be done,
& even though time
goes on & routine
becomes the norm,
underneath there sometimes
hangs the doubt
& sorrow that
the pain could have
been diverted but
you cannot have
your cake &
eat it too,
it would be a strange
life if so.

SUNDAY MORNING

Sunday morning
& the people walking, drifting
down the tree-lined pathways
thinking softly of the
spring coming leaving
winter behind,
flowers cropping up
smells & sounds of summer
soon to be.
Sunday morning
& the quiet tells of
hands-in-pockets-nothing
left to do,
early sun rises floats across
a turquoise sky
& looks for something to happen,
but it doesn't because it's
Sunday morning
& nothing is supposed to happen,
hearts beat slowly conversation
floating on clean fresh air,
not even a rustle in the leaves,
trees too wait some happening
but its a holiday.
Sunday morning
& the rush is gone,
the week past with all
it's headaches,
stress & rushing round
has left this day alone
to reflect on it all,
some are bored & twiddle
their thumbs waiting
for Monday when they can
rush & work & get the headaches,
(at least they have something to do).
Sunday morning
it was made to sit & ponder,
walk on roads & looking yonder

off of cliffs boats in water
blue on blue,
not a time for problems,
troubles, worries,
those are better left
for another day.

WITCH SHIPMATE

Across from me the witch in white
sits cross-legged in proud repose,
I see her clearly through
half-baked eyes,
hidden from all around by glasses
darkened for the sun,
"She's the lazy one!" I think
as she slouches back on deck
& waits the commands
(she really wants to
do the commanding herself),
not a smile or even a hint
creases those lips of hers,
(to do so would be to drop down
off her lofty perch),
better to gaze far off in pretended
importance.
I'm wondering what's worse than a
know-it-all who doesn't
know anything & while we sweat
she watches but does not deign
to lend a hand,
all the day the frown continues,
she doesn't really want to be here,
just wants the day to end,
while the rest of us are learning
to scramble, tack & gybe,
to haul on sheets & read the wind,
she takes the helm
with the know-it-all face,
but gets hit with blasts
that heel us over,
& terror makes her gasp for help,
we look on & wonder
that if she knew
half as much
as her face portrayed,
we wouldn't be terring around
grabbing lines & keeping sails

from flapping madly,
we'd be calmly sailing
with the whistling wind
& heading straight
on our desired course,
but the face is back
when things are right again
& when we dock
it's time for snugging down,
but where is she
while we scrub decks
& tuck away all the loose lines?
gone off to talk to friends ashore,
gone off to frown at someone else,
but maybe she's gone for good,
we sure don't want to be
shipmates again
with the likes of her.

A BURDEN THE HAND

You suffer your beliefs
& your feelings,
others see it differently
& do not understand,
you suffer for your thoughts,
the movements of your heart,
your emotions -
you suffer for your position,
the way you've gone in life,
others stand distantly
& judge the way you move
& somewhere down inside your being
the pain arises
because you know
they judge the action
& don't know the inner
working of the heart,
the motive for the way you've gone,
you suffer for this path
because you strike out alone,
all friendship & affection
falls away,
family, friends & kin
wave a cold farewell
as you step into the blizzard
& the fog of a strange
& unknown future.
You suffer for a step,
a heartbeat
that has changed lives,
others view it in despair
& wring their hands in dismay,
shake their heads buried
in their hands
& pass a judgement
that affects you deep inside,
you suffer & they never know
the sorrow & the pain
they only see the outward face,

the warpaint & the battle cry
& never see the broken heart
hidden down below,
& so you suffer on a lonely road
that takes you far away,
from all the things so well known
& established long before,
these others keep
their guard held high
& push you ever farther away
& never know you suffer,
you fret & wear away,
plunge headlong into
an uncertain world of
new faces, hopes & dreams
& don't look back
at the battlefield
for fear
that there is more
suffering still at hand.

HOW CAN I DESCRIBE

How can I describe
the way I feel
& what I see
when down inside I look
at her?
What happens when the
heart looks up to find
that she is there
with smile in hand
& welcome reaching
to my soul?
How can words be good enough
to tell that, though it may
make no logic sense,
the feeling down from deep inside
is good enough & strong enough
to feed & clothe me -
keep me strong & happy -
fill me with a sense of worth?

NIGHT TIME WRITER

I stand in readiness
& await the midnight star
that promises to be here,
I need the inspiration
& I need the spirit flowing,
I am able & waiting
for it's entrance in my heart,
the clock is ticking
& quiet lies in layers all around,
any moment in the darkness
I can feel it coming
& it shoots down into the light
& spills out onto pages.
I lay awake & feel the pressure,
hear the sounds of nearby night,
coloured deeply by the stars
& brightly smelling
by the summer breeze,
listen softly for the footsteps,
maybe only whispered voices
coming to me through the haze,
pushing out the thoughts of
daytimes's thousands of decisions
whose children are the little jobs
that fill the eight hour slot.
I fill a fountain pen with anger,
let it spread out it's magic
on paper white & clean,
let it burn it's holes in pages
ripe for anything at all,
anything we desire to throw at it,
any face we love to hate
& anyone we need to hurt,
the ink can fill the pores of paper
& can reach the faintest ear
if it's heard & understood,
it does more good than hate or fear.
I toss & turn & soak the sheets,
pace the rooms in drunken slumber

til the pins & needles &
the restlessness disappear,
fall down lifeless hoping for
sleep in wavelets to roll over
but stop the brain
from cross-examining
& digging out every well-known fact,
seeing every worn-out face
that crossed my path today
& will cross again tomorrow.
I wasn't planning for things
to turn out this way
but this is life with all it's
twists & turns,
you can sit like stable cowboy,
motionless & stiff to all life's ways
or you can reach out for the limits
(which are only in your mind),
your craft or art or inspiration
(whatever it may be)
is your expression & your life
& will come knocking
though you turn it all away,
some will hide it under carpets
& some will push it in the attic,
some will take it to the garbage,
destroy it in some other way,
but then in the lone night waking
comes the knocking
of this inspiration
who is not to be denied
& fill your heart & head
with whispers louder than the dead,
keeps you walking, taking
walks in empty rooms,
telling out those little things
that must be said.
Some have laughed & mocked
at those who sought

43

to snare the moment,
grab that thought contained
within their head,
paint it, write it, play it loudly
while the "normal" man sits idle
watching with his face of doubt,
he can't hear the music playing,
the harmonies two-part filling
every section of your head,
he can't see the colours
contained in patterns
swiftly swirling
through those curtains of your mind,
he only sees the greys & things
that "normal" folks have done
& worries that his job's done right
& the car's gas tank
has a satisfied appetite.
It is only twenty years but seems
like someone else's life,
how could all those things I did
not be some dream I had last night?
there was sweat & laughter
& regrets
& all the chances & opportunities,
seemed like they were so ripe then
when youth was on my side,
I took it all so fearlessly
& never cared a bit
if anything ever happened,
(but maybe a lot was just
inexperience & naivete).
We pass those years only
& take it a day at a time
& then those days are gone,
the youth & golden opportunities
have turned to age & rust,
the regrets that seemed
so little then

now become a daily complaint
& you live those things
& fear those things
because this life is galloping
on through that dark night
& not one single regret
or complaint or sigh
will change it's silent flight.

Whatever's gone is gone,
the fire has licked the pages clean,
they can't be formed again,
the rust has turned them red
& eaten them clean through,
the theives have sold them
to someone on the streets,
the wind has blown them
page by page to the corners
of the earth,
the moths have chewed
& digested them,
their ashes have been spread
right across the land,
they are only a memory
buried deep underground
& best forgotten
because each glimpse of them
in retrospect
brings another pang of bitterness
& another day's regrets.

ROUGH STONES

Some of us find life to be
hard & full of rough stones
that need to be cleared,
every corner has it's burden
around it,
every pathway has it's stump
& running headlong breezily
feeling joyful summer laughing
is as foreign as the lands
across the sea,
some of us are born with thorns
in place of bones
& feel the pricks on every turn,
with every movement of the day
events of life bring no happiness,
just confusion with harsh realities,
some were born to turn tail & run
when sun comes beaming round
the clouds
to brighten every damp rag in life,
& instead of soaking
in it's warm rays
find shelter underneath the four
wet walls of cellars down below,
curtained from the scrapes & falls
that make up every
full-lived day in life.

UNDERNEATH IT ALL

Underneath the shining stars
the world turns on
& the voices ring
like bells in church
& the chimes are heard for miles,
you cannot get away from the chimes.
Underneath the covers
in the middle of the night
the warmth & privacy like
a penitentiary cell, close & secure
keep walls up straight
& strangers from the door.
Underneath it all
when all is said & done
when people have passed
their judgements
& said their piece,
spoken last words & given advice,
their love remains the same
(they cannot fool me).
Underneath the burning bridges
memories linger & gently fade,
people in their mongrel colours
all play the same stale game
but some hold high
their flag of pride,
others lay low & let their hearts
reach out in unfeigned love.

SHORT TERM

The thirsting ache of brain & heart
together weave a sorry tale,
years will erode these things I'm sure
or build them to a grander scale.

A million days of empty sun
like rings on a hardy maple tree
will pass like tankers in the night
& never mean a thing to me.

It is only moments like this one
that ever stick around,
always when we're warm & cuddling
the moments fade like fleeting sound.

But pain is what this world's about,
hurting & sorrow are nothing new,
every silver lining has a cloud
& death is never far from view.

So just get used to life's dull ache,
to angry faces & crying too,
heartaches always have a way
of catching up with you.

IF I WERE A BLIND MAN

If I were a blind man
I would still enjoy your scent,
follow it's trails around the house
& follow you wherever you go.

If I were a blind man
I would still know where you are,
sense your presence everywhere
& lay beside you still.

If I were a blind man
I would feel your love for me,
it could not be hid by darkness
or blotted out by night.

If I were a blind man
I would listen for your footsteps,
always keep you close at hand
just one step ahead of me.

ROLLER COASTER

I am glad
the emotional roller coaster ride
is over,
It was hard to understand
at the time,
heaving up & down in indecision,
rocking back & forth like
a little boat in a heavy sea,
first one way & then another,
drawn here by this smitten heart
& that way by responsibility,
turned off here by reacting people
& spurred on there by
those who saw it differently,
I am glad
those days have flown
leaving peace & rest
at last,
decisions made bring rest,
things nailed down
don't fly away
with every wind.

What made the great ones great
was that they were larger than life,
they could not be little men
like you or I.
What made the great ones great
was the awe they made you feel
because you knew you were no match
with giants like them.
What made the great ones great
is that they seemed inhuman,
too inhuman to do the things
that you & I do.
What made the great ones great
was the way the world viewed them,
you could see the deep respect
in their eyes.
What made the great ones great
was their ageless durability,
it was as if they had
always been here
from the beginning.
What made the great ones great
was their recognizablity,
you knew them well & they knew you,
like your family.

MORNING BONES

Early morning & my bones are aching,
I roll in tent on hard rock floor
& each bone in his place
starts singing,
one by one they cry their chorus
& in disharmony
they "all-together-now"
throughout my whole being.
Rising is a chore with all these
enemies pointing
their sharp sticks at me
making every movement agony,
needing air to breathe lungs gasp
& make the ribcage heave
causing spasms of pain,
rolling out of bed the bones rebel
& try to hold me still
or they will start their singing,
grating, out-of-tune noises
that drive me hands-on-ears
far from my tent & my bed
which is glad to see me go.

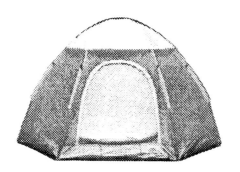

53

EMPTY HEART

Whispered teardrops sneaking down
somewhere in the night,
no one hears & no one dreams
that they are there
or what they mean,
could it be that somewhere someone
feels the way I do tonight?
if it's so, they're miles away
& unable to enter in,
touch the heart
& feel the pain.
What makes the night so long
is the darkness,
thick & black & all around,
silent thoughts of sorrow
drift in unseen clouds,
clinging & holding on.
Worn & weary from the night
of darkness & the thoughts
& dreams of doubt,
morning brings some reason
to the long ordeal,
but the empty heart & hollow shell
still knows that life
with all it's ups & downs
remains the same.

VISITING HOURS

Guess you feel
a little strange
when you think
of who I am &
what I've done,
peering through these bars
I see a piece
of yesterday's life
& what I could have been.
You look so "normal",
dressed so nice
like everyday is Sunday,
you must feel secure
knowing you are "normal"
& everybody likes you.
I feel the coldness of
this cell sometimes,
& feel my crime nagging me
& trying to overwhelm me,
but I run the race
of life too - like you
& have no regrets because
I did what was right
for the time.
you will never understand, I know,
your "visit" ends & you must go.

MEMORIES

Memories of kids & dogs
& people disciplining
each & every one,
years of watching people go,
all their characteristics
& idiosyncrasies,
each with his own way
of making his motor go,
keeping it running,
& then the kids grow
& the parents too
from crawling babies
with bonnets & white shoes
to young ladies with
shy smiles & long dresses,
fretful, teething babies,
restless & tired soon become
tall young men with
awkward movements,
some of them are memories
burned in & etched boldly
& will not go away,
sometimes they bring tears
& sometimes happiness,
all are part of the past,
a part of the web of life
woven from parts
& components that create
a whole & complete being,
some remembered, some forgotten,
some learned & some unlearned,
memories like pages
from a long book,
thick with dust
& pungent with mold,
taken from a shelf at lonely times,
the story read again
& again.

THE TURQUOISE STONE

The fear came gradually,
then in spasms far & wide
& running like some fraidy cat,
not thinking, seeing or hearing,
just struck with terror
through & through
until that moment when
I reached your twinkling
jewellry box,
inside was the turquoise stone.

It didn't matter what they said,
the mud they slung,
the way they looked,
the arrows stuck & the blood flowed
but the pain reached a point
& then diminished,
I thought carefully & realized
that they could not really touch me
for round my neck
was the turquoise stone.

The farewells came slowly,
each & every one had come
to bid his own adieu,
boxes packed & things gathered,
I searched corners of the house,
collected in last memories
& looking back I trembled slightly
for on the table
was the turquoise stone.

Friends may have gone their way
& not have needed me,
they have their world
that keeps them strong,
they have each other for security,
I may be standing far from them,
far from that world I knew so well,
but today I know I'm not alone
for I still have the turquoise stone.

57

WOOD HOUSE HOME

It was
an old house with real wood
walls & shelves & stairs
& everything creaked,
but everything was warm
to the touch
& we loved it all,
the smell & the feel & the sound
of it all,
wallpaper on wallpaper
& linoleum on linoleum
& paint on paint,
layers thick,
scrubbed & washed & still old,
it felt so warm,
even on cold winter nights
when wind whistled through
cracks in the walls,
candles flickered & cast
strange shadows
on flowered wallpaper,
it was really home,
down in our hearts
& in our blood.

DAMPER ON LIFE

You are always,
seeing life your way,
my way is not your way
so you put a damper on it,
taking life & seeing it through
eyes that see your dreams,
not others,
so you put a damper on life,
we try & fail because,
you dampen it,
you take,
enthusiasm out of it,
it hurts,
because failure is not fun,
but underneath we know,
we are not failures,
it is only your estimation,
it is only you putting a damper
on this life.
We will rise above your dampness,
the sun will shine on us,
dry us out
& make us smile in victory.

SORROW

Sorrow comes quickly
when life changes course,
sometimes you are not ready
for the change inside of you,
when it comes you stagger on,
try to make life work
the way it used to do.

Now you are out of step,
the people march along side of you,
one by one & two by two,
but you are feeling pain & wondering
if they do too.
But your pain is unique,
who can understand?
it sits inside & rumbles
like a teapot trying to explode.

Sorrow sticks around
when you sleep & when you wake,
when you eat & when you work,
you take it with you all your days,
& you don't forget it
though you live a hundred years.

ACKNOWLEDGEMENT

Nothing here reminds me of you,
all your pictures are gone,
the past is only memories,
I do not think about you,
every step draws me away,
I do not walk backwards,
a new world opens up,
there were times
that were warm & happy but
things have changed,
bridges have been crossed,
I walk from room to room
& do not see you,
I do not think back
to those times long ago,
they are too far off &
lots of things
did not work out
the way they were supposed to
& now a new day has dawned
on me
& I walk new worlds
with someone new,
but sometimes I turn
& tip my hat to you.

FICKLE FRIENDS

Still can't get used
to the fact
that they loved me
& now they hate me
for this little thing I've done,
strange that a brother
can love you & hug you
& then in a moment of time
can turn cold
& ignore you,
see you & not talk,
know you're there
& not call,
run when the thought
of you comes up.

This is no brother of mine
who loves me one moment
& not the next,
this is no friend
who loves me out of
one side of his face only
while the other waits
for me to fall.

LIVING ON LOVE

It is the power
& the force
that pushes, pulls,
propels us forward,
motivates us to move,
breathe, function,
carry on in life,
this warm throbbing
that comes from
far within,
that makes us smile
at unlikely times
& look across the room
at one another
with knowing glances,
it is a life
& it's whole reason for being
is love,
you can sometimes
see it,
feel it in the air
like airwaves,
transmitting sounds
& thoughts & feelings,
because it is alive,
just as alive
all living, breathing beings,
as heartbeats
& lungs gasping air,
it keeps each morning
starting up
& each evening closing down,
each moment of the day
ticking by,
it is love
& if it ever stops
the whole being will
shut down & quit
& the life will ebb away
& will be no more,

because the force has gone,
batteries dead,
reason for being
faded away,
cold & still lying
corpses in the empty night.

THE MOVE

Can't put my finger on
exactly
the reason why
& the motive for
this change of life,
something back in lengths
of time
propelled the thoughts & mind
& put a seed in that ground
that grew
until today it came to be
that this move came about
naturally.
You never really know
when faced with arguments
& questions
about what made you move
& how could it be?
You stumble & dig back
in your mind
to try & find something
logical & reasonable
to tell them
& yet you come out looking
sometimes so bad,
opinions of you stick
& you feel like running
from it all,
but when you think
& quietly repose,
you see some light
at the far-off end of the tunnel,
some things make sense,
some reason comes,
& though you scrape it up
from here & there,
a small beginning emerges
& you know that what you did
you'd do again,

you can't put your finger on it
but in time you know
it will all be well.

you can't put your finger on it
but in time you know
it will all be well.

MAGNETS

I would jump the walls
& scale the fences
for a chance to be with you,
I would climb the mountains
& roam the hills
for a chance to see you,
no hurdle & no hedge
could come between us,
we could never be apart,
even if they'd separate us
one world from another,
a country east &
a country west,
there are no wings or wheels
invented that could put us
together faster
because like magnets
we are drawn & pulled
from all directions
back together again.

EXPLANATIONS

One day you get tired
of all the explanations,
you wake the new day
from it's twisted position,
shake it's wrinkles off
& stand as firm as possible,
one day you look for new horizons,
newer faces that never know
the past & all it's traces,
not really running but maybe
hiding just a little,
they can never know from looking
how many hurts you've
left behind
or how many little thorns still
prickle just underneath the skin,
one day you want to chuck it all
deep in the ocean far away,
let the west wind blow it's
brains out,
bring some fairer breezes
from another land,
fill you with some fresh-picked
answers that require
no explanations.

ONE OF THEM

You're one of them
& it fits you real good,
you do the job well,
you carry it off fine,
you fit right in
to that other crowd of them
& they all look like you
& you look like them,
I used to be
one of them,
I looked & felt like them,
tried to be like them,
but underneath I guess
I couldn't make the grade,
but you look good,
it fits you like a glove,
you smile like them
& walk like them,
you live like them
because you are them
& they are you,
I am glad today that I
am not one of them,
I do not have to jump like them
or talk like them,
I can be just as I please
& not feel like I did
when I was
one of them.

HATRED

Hatred scares me
because it seems to be
the driving force
that makes
the world go round.
It gnaws inside of you
til it comes out in violence,
it explodes like dynamite
& causes pain,
& a world full of bloodshed
is the result of
my little fist
of hatred.

LADY IN A WHEELCHAIR

Lady in a wheel chair smiling,
I feel sorry for her
in one way
& happy for her
in another,
sorry for her because
she can't get around
like the rest of us,
happy for her because
she has risen above it
& maybe found a side
of life
that we have not seen.

REASONS TO RUN

There comes times
when you want
ends to meet &
reasons to run,
you want to be settled
safely beneath
a comforting sun,
there comes times
when you want
it all to end,
a new beginning,
to start again,
you want to put your feet
on solid ground,
something unmoving,
a future safe &
a future sound,
you want to stop running,
start living,
check the horizon,
take on new things
with a hand that's giving
& a heart that's feeling,
touching the pulse
of the real world.
There comes times
when you want
to forget the past,
call it a day,
whatever happened
didn't last,
let it go & let it be,
today's dawn brings
something new,
for tomorrow we will
wait & see.

RIGHTEOUS DAYS

Way back when,
you wouldn't think
of doing this
or doing that,
it wouldn't have done,
wouldn't have been right
back in those righteous days.
It felt better
to wear the right clothes
& say the right things
& not do the things
that everybody did
for the sake of being right
back in those righteous days.
It seemed as though
we were the only ones
to know what's right & wrong,
others seemed so ordinary
doing whatever felt good
or whatever seemed right,
they never reached the plane
that we were on
back in those righteous days.
We lived in
our very own world
devoid of any & all who
didn't see life
our way,
we had our special way
of doing what we did
& it didn't matter who
understood or not
back in those righteous days.
Back then you said & did
the things you knew you should,
your own crowd liked it,
others thought it strange,
but it fit the time

& seemed to keep us satisfied
above & beyond the common people
who could not see our ways
which never changed
back in those righteous days.
Today so much has changed,
ideas & times are all so new,
people have come & gone,
things they did have passed away,
bad things now are not so bad,
unacceptable things now are
accepted & taken for granted,
old time cobwebs are brushed away
& only a few can remember
back to those righteous days.

ROOMS

Echoed down in curtained rooms
somewhere within your mind
feelings grow & spawn that maybe
the legs have been removed from you
& you shuffle Quazamoto-like
from place to place wondering why
people seem to want to clap
themselves up in groups & share
their laughter one-on one.
You feel alone hanging from
this flagpole flying for all
the world to see,
it is not a pretty sight,
all these years you've worked
for something that seems now
to belong to others
& you hang lost, lonely & afraid
& you recline back to those
curtained rooms of safety,
silence & sanity.

I OWE MY HEART

I owe my heart
to you,
it belongs to you
& if I waver or
fall away,
I remember that
I owe my heart
to you.
I owe my heart
to you,
it has your name
engraved on it,
if someone comes
& calls to me,
they don't know that
I owe my heart
to you.
I owe my heart
to you,
you have given
yours to me
& mine belongs
to you,
It can't be bought
or sold because
I owe my heart
to you.
I owe my heart
to you,
you hold it in
your hand
& when I'm far away
my love will whisper
& tell me that
I owe my heart
to you.

I owe my heart
to you,
no one deserves it more,
you will treat it kind
& make me glad that
I owe my heart
to you.

NIGHT SKY

A silvery moon lay sulking over
the lawns & fields of home
& the stars waved one by one,
a few lonely clouds crept silently
past like phantoms in the night
& a still, peaceful feeling fell
over all creation.

A reddish planet sent it's glow
all the way to earth,
frozen in the sky like a
thousand years before,
it's colours blending suitably
with the others in the sky,
& silent movements here & there
like life in a summer pond,
made the ceiling feel like
a neon lighted sign.

Like the ocean bottom fathoms down,
the night sky holds it's mystery,
the farther out we reach it seems
the more baffled we become,
like the moving beds of kelp
& the shadowy schools of fish
that fascinate our curious minds,
the wonders of the universe too
hold us tightly in their grip.

CHICKEN COOPS

Up on a hill
a low grey cloud grows slowly
& steadily
moving like a growth from
top to bottom,
where a wall of green once grew
it is now cleared away
& a long line of chicken coops
stand in an even row
like soldiers going to war,
all built the same &
all the same colour,
they will soon be filled with people
anxious for a home,
a place of their own,
like hamsters tightly
squeezed into their cages,
it wouldn't take a
Frank Lloyd Wright to design
chicken coops like that,
they are designed for convenience -
how many college students
can you fit into a phone booth?

YOU ARE NO CRIMINAL

You should not feel
that loving me
makes you a criminal,
your love expresses
what is down
in your heart,
you reach out & touch me,
others may see it
& then you feel bad,
but you are not wrong,
we are no criminals
just because we love
each other,
your can lift your head
up high
& be proud because
you love,
& because
you are loved.